piano / vocal / guitar

best of BILLY PRESTON

Cover photo © David Redfern/Redferns/Retna LTD.

ISBN 978-1-4234-6189-0

HAL•LEONARD®
CORPORATION
7777 W. BLUEMOUND RD. P.O. BOX 13819 MILWAUKEE, WI 53213

Visit Hal Leonard Online at
www.halleonard.com

FANCY LADY

Words and Music by BILLY PRESTON
and SYREETA WRIGHT

Male: Fan - cy la - dy is mas-quer-ad - ing_____ with a heart that no-bod-y can cheat.

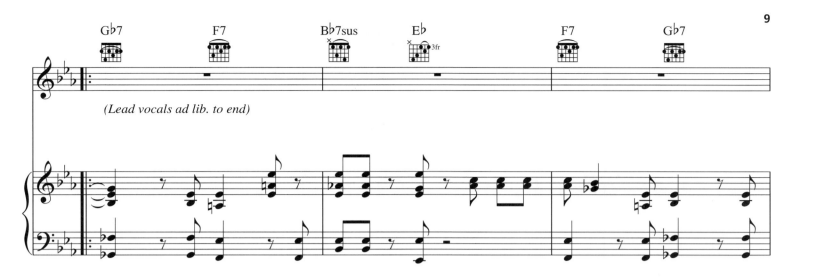

(Lead vocals ad lib. to end)

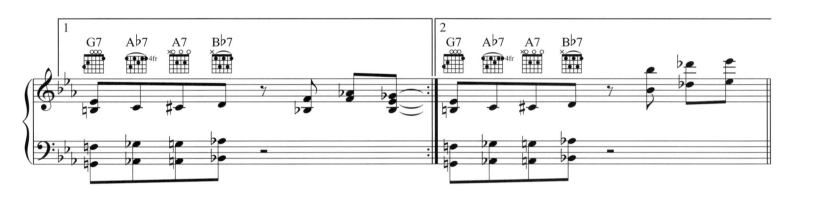

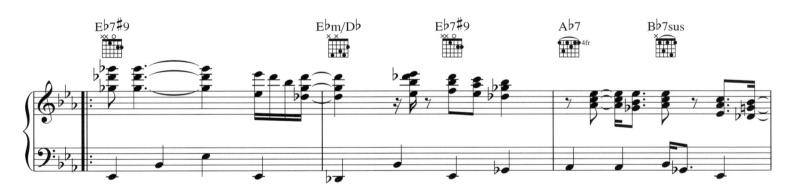

Repeat and Fade

Optional Ending

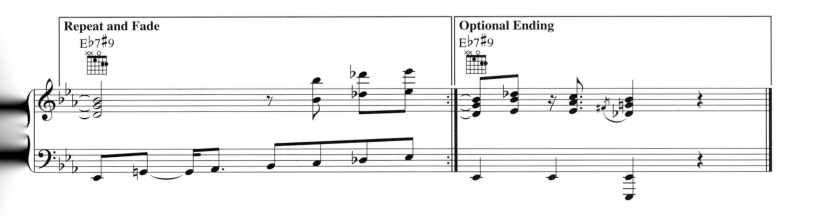

GET BACK

Words and Music by JOHN LENNON
and PAUL McCARTNEY

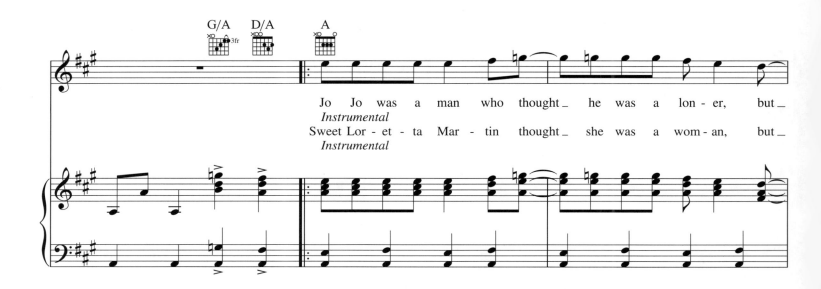

Jo Jo was a man who thought _ he was a lon-er, but _
Instrumental
Sweet Lor-et-ta Mar-tin thought _ she was a wom-an, but _
Instrumental

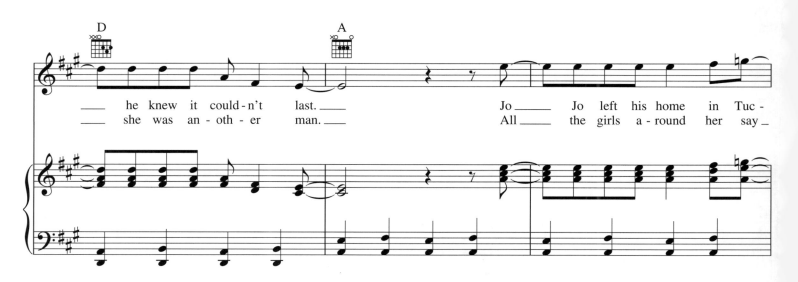

_ he knew it could-n't last. _
_ she was an-oth-er man. _
Jo _ Jo left his home in Tuc-
All _ the girls a-round her say

12

I WROTE A SIMPLE SONG

Words and Music by BILLY PRESTON
and JOSEPH GREENE

Now it sounds like a sym - pho - ny.

wrote it for you. ___ It's yours ___ and mine, _____ girl. _

Instrumental solos ad lib.

I'M REALLY GONNA MISS YOU

Words and Music by
BILLY PRESTON

LET IT BE

Words and Music by JOHN LENNON
and PAUL McCARTNEY

NOTHING FROM NOTHING

Words and Music by BILLY PRESTON
and BRUCE FISHER

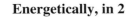

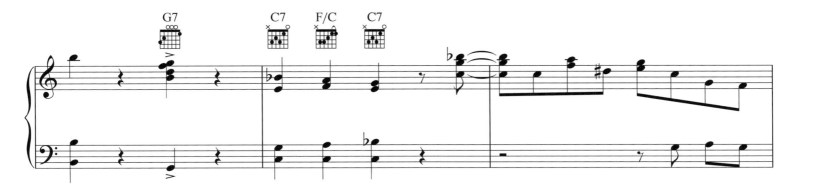

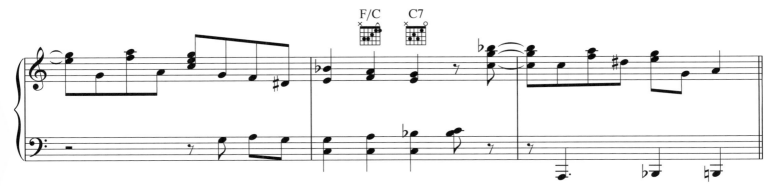

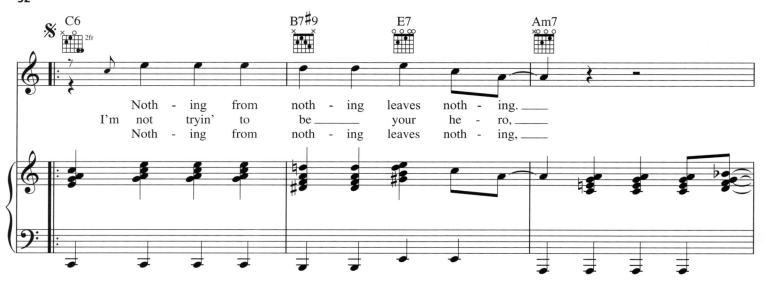

Noth - ing from noth - ing leaves noth - ing. ____
I'm not tryin' to be ____ your he - ro, ____
Noth - ing from noth - ing leaves noth - ing, ____

You got - ta have some - thing if you wan - na be with me. ____
'cause that ____ ze - ro, ____ is too ____ cold ____ for ____ me. ____
and I'm ____ not ____ stuff - in', be - lieve ____ you ____ me. ____

____ Noth - ing from noth - ing leaves
____ I'm not tryin' to be ____ your high -
____ Don't you re - mem - ber? I told

OUTA-SPACE

Words and Music by BILLY PRESTON
and JOSEPH GREENE

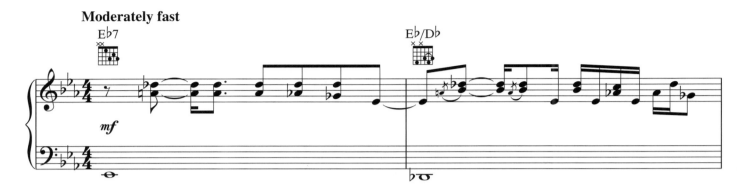

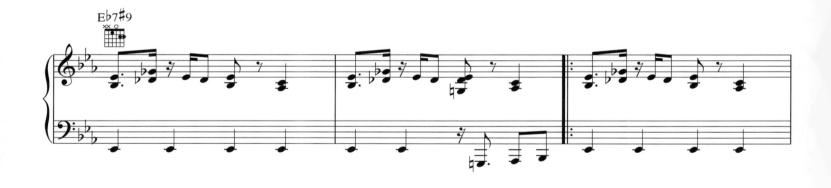

SPACE RACE

Words and Music by
BILLY PRESTON

Moderately fast

STRUTTIN'

Words and Music by BILLY PRESTON,
GEORGE JOHNSON and LOUIS JOHNSON

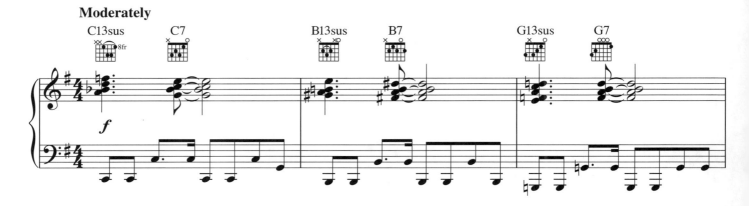

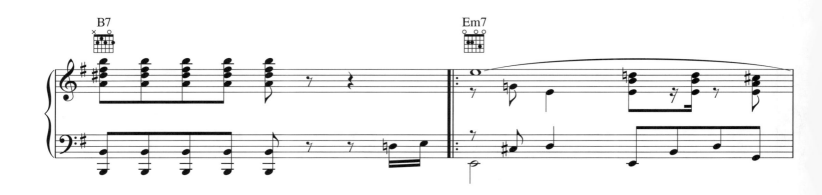

THAT'S THE WAY GOD PLANNED IT

Words and Music by
BILLY PRESTON

WILL IT GO ROUND IN CIRCLES

Words and Music by BILLY PRESTON
and BRUCE FISHER

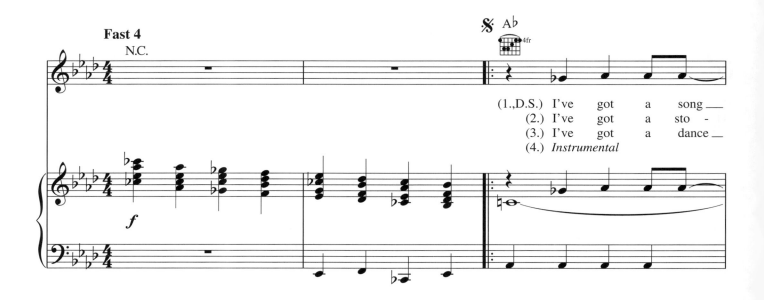

(1.,D.S.) I've got a song ___
(2.) I've got a sto -
(3.) I've got a dance ___
(4.) Instrumental

___ I ain't got no mel - o - dy. ___
- ry, ain't got no mor - al. _____
___ I ain't got no steps. _____

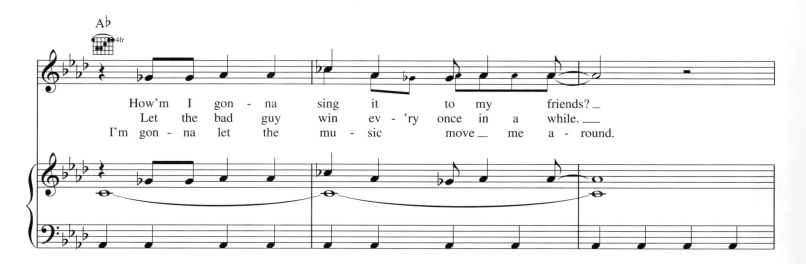

How'm I gon - na sing it to my friends? _
Let the bad guy win ev - 'ry once in a while. __
I'm gon - na let the mu - sic move ___ me a - round.

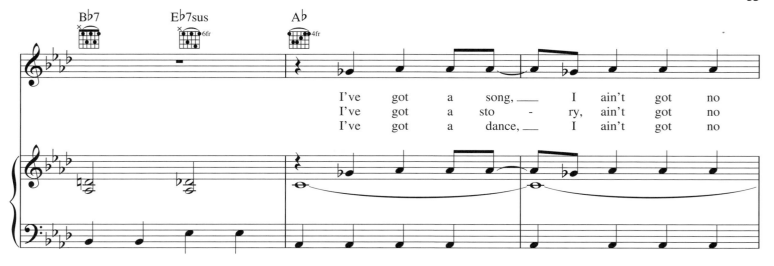

I've got a song, ___ I ain't got no
I've got a sto - ry, ___ ain't got no
I've got a dance, ___ I ain't got no

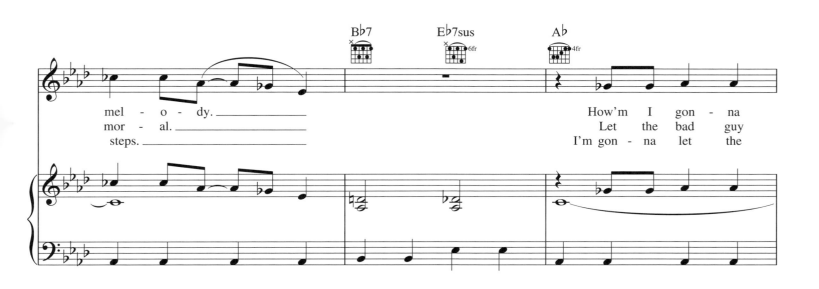

mel - o - dy. ___
mor - al. ___
steps. ___

How'm I gon - na
Let the bad guy
I'm gon - na let the

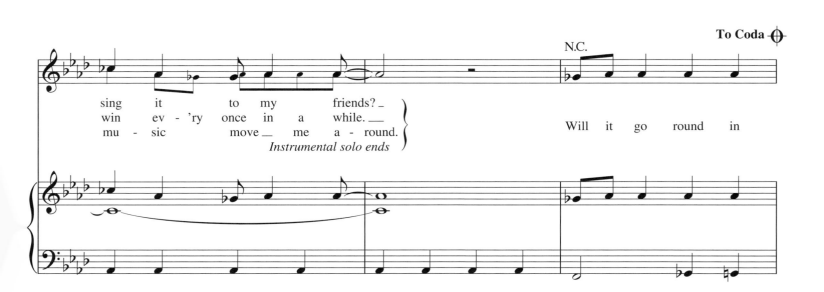

sing it to my friends? ___
win ev - 'ry once in a while. ___
mu - sic move ___ me a - round.

Instrumental solo ends

Will it go round in

53

To Coda ⊕

N.C.

WITH YOU I'M BORN AGAIN

Words by CAROL CONNORS
Music by DAVID SHIRE

Male: Come, bring me your soft - ness. Com - fort me through all this mad - ness. Wom - an, don't you know, with you I'm born a - gain.

Female: Come

YOU ARE SO BEAUTIFUL

Words and Music by BILLY PRESTON
and BRUCE FISHER

Moderately slow, expressively

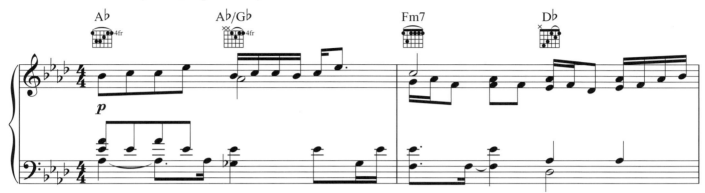

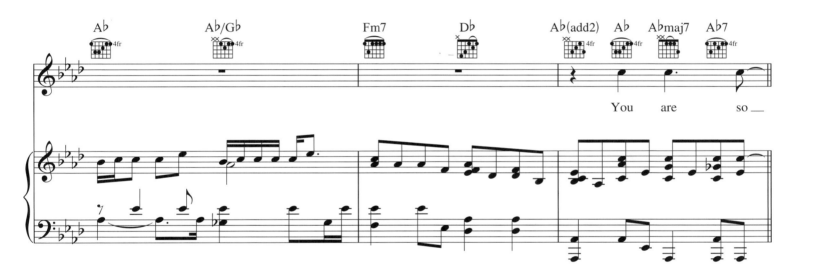

You are so ___

___ beau - ti - ful ___   to

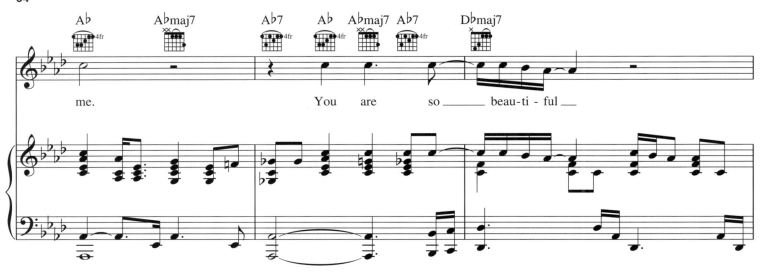

me.
You are so _____ beau-ti-ful _____

to me.
Can't you

see? _____

You're ev-'ry-thing I
You're ev-'ry-thing I

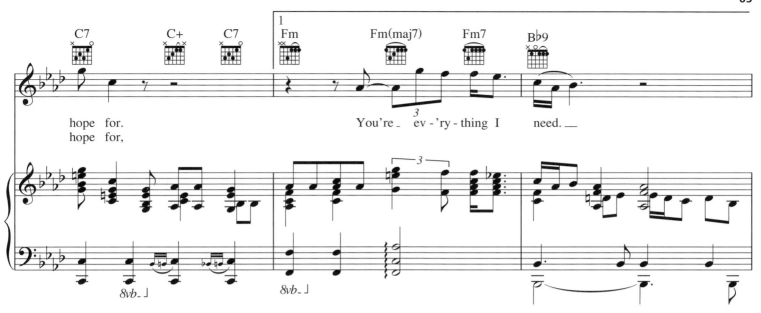

hope for.
hope for,

You're ev-'ry-thing I need. —

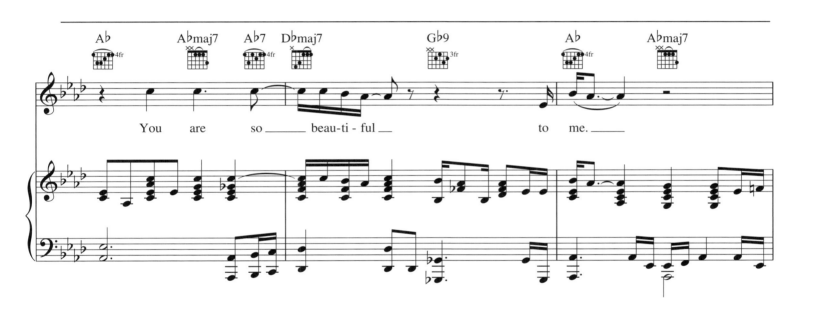

You are so ___ beau-ti-ful ___ to me. ___

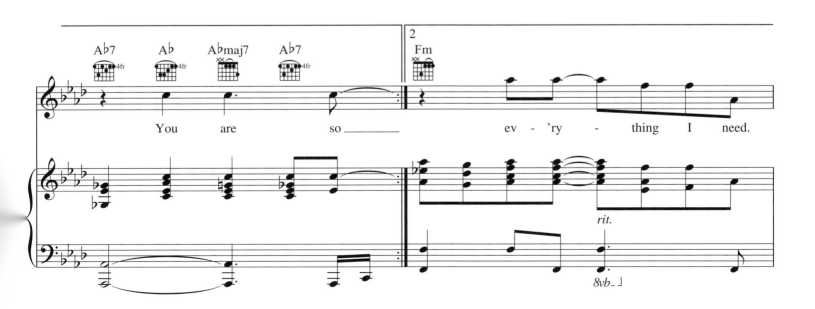

You are so ___ ev-'ry-thing I need.

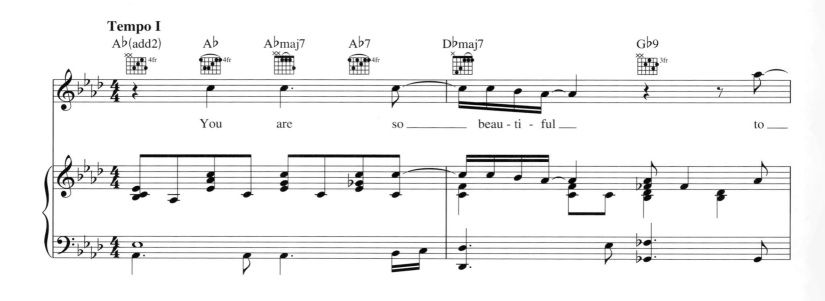

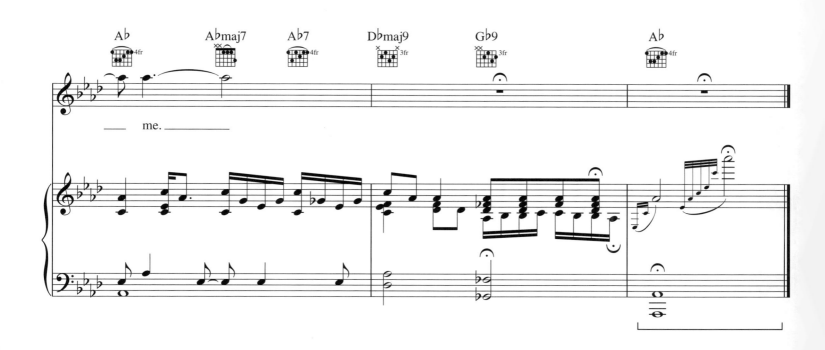

YOU'RE SO UNIQUE

Words and Music by BILLY PRESTON
and JOSEPH GREENE

Hee, __ yeah, _____ girl. _____